One deck

Laundrette

Grill Room Bar

One Deck Shop

down

up

Beauty Salon

Barbers Shop

One Deck Lido

Suite Suite Suite Suite Suite Suite Suite

Two deck

Forward Lobby

Bank

Bureau

Midships Lobby

Doctor

After Lobby

Engineer

up
dn

Suite Suite Suite Suite

Three deck

Synagogue

up
dn

Four deck

Five deck

Six deck

Treat room

Bathroom

Massage

Swimming pool

Laundrette

Gents changing room

Seven deck

Sauna

Gymnasium

Swimming pool

Key to Symbols

Bed uppers A and B
lowers 1 and 2)
Settee bed
Bath.
Shower
Washbasin
Refrigerator
Closet
Toilet
Bidet
Wardrobe
Dressing, table or
chest of drawers

D1493076

By the same author

Night Ferry (Jersey Artists Ltd, 1985)
Dream Voyages (Jersey Artists Ltd, 1989)

Ocean Liners
Past and Present

Queen Elizabeth 2

A unique view of QE2 during her 1994 refit in dry dock at Blohm & Voss in Hamburg. The bulbous bow was, at the time of construction, one of the most advanced points of design in the ship, creating the sort of wave-form through which a ship passes most easily. *Niall Clutton/MET Studio Ltd, London*

Ocean Liners
Past and Present

Queen Elizabeth 2

A magnificent millennium

Gary C. Buchanan

Past & Present Publishing Ltd

© Gary C. Buchanan 1995

First published in January 1996

British Library Cataloguing in Publication Data

A catalogue record for this book is available from the British Library

ISBN 1 85895 122 4

Past & Present Publishing Ltd
Unit 5
Home Farm Close
Church Street
Wadenhoe
Peterborough PE8 5TE
Tel/fax (01832) 720440

Printed and bound in Great Britain

Cover illustrations

Front, top The drama of a morning sunrise highlights QE2 to perfection as she sails towards Southampton to complete 1,000 voyages. During a crossing passengers rediscover an enigmatic quality so rare in today's 'hurry up' lifestyle - time. This most magical, most glamorous feature that QE2 offers is the very essence of a crossing. Five days of detachment, of languor and indolence, free from cares, responsibilities and duties. Passengers succumb to the gentle rise and fall of the great hull, the soft creaking of the cabin walls, while down below the steady shudder of the ship's massive engines is testimony to awesome power. In a world where time is in meagre supply, being 2,000 miles out to sea, surrounded by luxury, is akin to membership of a very exclusive club - a peripatetic nirvana - where the sole concept of time is marked daily at noon with a long, melancholy toot on the ship's whistle, while sunrises seem to spread, unencumbered, across the edge of the world. *Cunard, London*

Front, below left *Queen Elizabeth 2* in 1969. The sleek profile was to change considerably over 1,000 voyages as additions were made to her superstructure. QE2's transatlantic service has been supported by those who are loyal to, or curious about, the grandeur of a more leisurely era. In fact, QE2 is far more comfortable than any of her Atlantic predecessors. The last greyhound of the Atlantic was given what will inevitably be the last of the busy, noisy, triumphant maiden receptions in New York Harbour. Early observations and appraisals were not unanimous. Some thought her to be a superb example of contemporary ocean liner design and decoration; others were deeply disappointed that she hardly resembled that earlier generation of wood-panelled passenger ships at all. Much like the *Queen Mary* and other famous liner of the Thirties, QE2 was at the vanguard of innovation; certainly she was a ship that had to be suited to the competitive and pressing demands of several decades of crossing and cruising. *Brian Price*

Front, below right Returning to service in August 1982, following her active service in the Falklands War, QE2 sported a pebble-grey hull and, for the first time, her funnel was painted in Cunard red with two black bands. The intention was to give her a new appearance after her return from trooping duties; however, the grey hull was very difficult to maintain in pristine condition, and some paint was always lost when using tugs or from close contact with dockside fenders. After a reasonable trial period, Cunard decided to revert to the original dark grey and QE2 was repainted in June 1983; however, the distinctive Cunard red and black colour scheme of the funnel was retained. Following the 1994 refit the hull was painted in a very dark royal blue and the 'racing stripe' added. Today, QE2 - the most fabled of modern liners - is truly majesty at sea. *Collection Peter Boyd-Smith at Cobwebs*

Back This wonderful study of QE2 at night was taken during the ship's last refit in the Blohm & Voss yard in Hamburg. QE2 is at her most noble by night: a thousand lights are reflected a thousand times as this city at sea forges across the oceans of the world with more than a star to steer her by. To witness QE2 sailing at night from her berth at Southampton in December or from New York in January as she begins a World Cruise is to witness one of the great wonders of the modern world, for QE2 is surely a vessel in excelsis.

There have been no fewer than five major transformations to QE2 in her illustrious career: Vosper Thorneycroft, Southampton, in 1972; Bethlehem Steel, Bayonne, New Jersey, in 1977; Lloyd Werft in Bremerhaven in both 1983 and 1987; and Blohm & Voss in Hamburg for the 1994 refit. There were also two minor refits at Blohm & Voss - in 1990 and 1992. No other ship in maritime history has metamorphosed so much during such an illustrious career - nor has any other vessel had as much money spent on her. As QE2 sails into the next millennium it is worth remembering that nothing made by man is granted such immortality as a ship. *Niall Clutton/MET Studio Ltd, London*

Acknowledgements

This book began with the sowing of the seed of an idea from June Applebee, Senior Librarian on board QE2 in the summer of 1994. Since then, with the help of innumerable people on both sides of the Atlantic who share my passion for the ship, I have been able to gather the necessary material to enable me to prepare this book. I would particularly like to extend my gratitude and heart-felt thanks to: Peter Bates, Peter Boyd-Smith, Captain John Burton-Hall, Geoffrey Coughtrey, Chris Cawte, David Chambers, Alan Chandler, Dianne Coles, John Duffy, Tony Fairhead, Eric Flounders, Michael Gallagher, Priscilla Hoye, John McNeece, Bill Miller, John Money, Brian Price, Jerry Singer, Christine Wares, Captain Ronald Warwick, David Williams, Captain Robin Woodall and Terry Yarwood. I am especially grateful to Niall Clutton for his excellent photography and to anybody I may have inadvertently omitted, please accept my sincere thanks.

When QE2 was launched, her two propellers were 19 feet in diameter and weighed 32 tons; each propeller had six blades. During the 1987 refit, when the steam turbines were replaced by diesel engines, new propellers were fitted. Now the 19 feet 8 inch diameter propellers have five variable-pitch blades providing maximum thrust. The pitch of the blades is controlled from either the Engine Room or from the Bridge. *Niall Clutton/MET Studio Ltd, London*

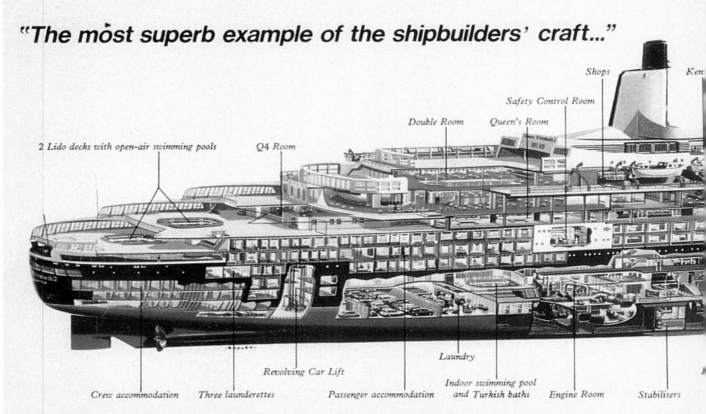

"The most superb example of the shipbuilders' craft..."

Shops *Ken*

Safety Control Room

Double Room *Queen's Room*

2 Lido decks with open-air swimming pools *Q4 Room*

Laundry

Revolving Car Lift

Crew accommodation *Three launderettes* *Passenger accommodation* *Indoor swimming pool and Turkish baths* *Engine Room* *Stabilisers*

QUEEN ELIZABETH 2 is 963 ft. long, and her beam at the widest point is 105 ft. Her draught is a moderate 32 ft. 6 ins. enabling her to enter many harbours previously closed to ships of her size. She stands 171 ft. 4 ins. out of the water.

Her gross tonnage is 65,863 tons, and she has 13 decks with a total deck space of 6,000 square yards.

The total complement is 920 crew members.

Only 70 seamen are needed to operate this the most highly mechanised of all the great ocean liners. Her 75-ton semi-balanced rudders are controlled by hydraulically operated steering gear. In turbulent seas two stabilisers reduce a lurching 20 degree roll to a mere unnoticeable three degrees. Berthing is made easier by two 1,000 h.p. bow-thrusters, and when the ship has to anchor three bow and one stern anchors each

weighing 12¾ tons and with 120 fathoms of cable ensure that she can ride the heaviest seas safely.

The engine room staff totals 94. They look after the two turbines each of which develops 110,000 h.p. Each turbine drives a 6-bladed, 19-ft. diameter, 31-ton propellor. At the normal cruising speed of 28.5 knots, the three boilers—which can produce 310,000 lbs. of steam per hour—consume 520 tons of fuel oil each day.

12

A cut-away profile of QE2 in 1969. Four of her 13 decks are constructed in aluminium - Upper Deck, Boat Deck, Sports Deck and Observation Deck. An epoxy-resin compound joins the aluminium superstructure with the steel hull, and steel rivets make the final bimetallic connection, preventing any corrosive electrolytic interaction. The saving in weight from the use of aluminium gave QE2 a 7-foot reduction in draft compared with the *Queen Mary* and *Queen Elizabeth*. This weight reduction also enabled QE2 to rise 13 decks high - one more than the old 'Queens' - more than compensating for the limits on length and beam that are imposed by constraints of the Panama and Suez canals. The present draft is normally 31 feet.

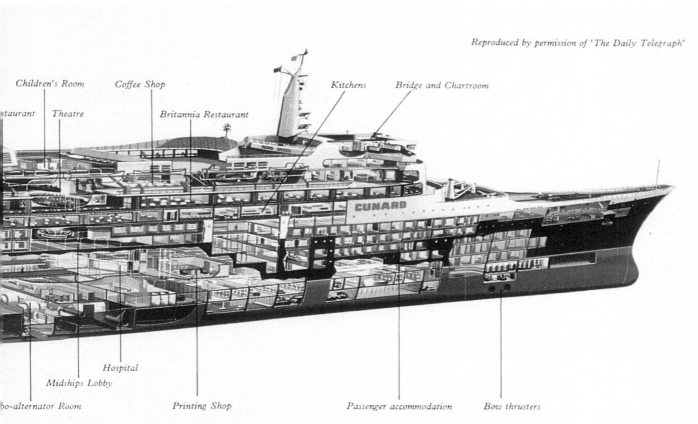

Children's Room   Coffee Shop   Kitchens   Bridge and Chartroom

...staurant   Theatre   Britannia Restaurant

CUNARD

Hospital

Midships Lobby

...o-alternator Room   Printing Shop   Passenger accommodation   Bow thrusters

Three turbo-alternators produce 5¼ megowatts of electricity, sufficient to supply a town the size of Southampton with all its light, heat and power requirements. This vast electrical output is needed to run the tremendous array of electrical equipment including air conditioning which is installed throughout the ship, the 22 lifts, the escalator which runs between the kitchen and the Britannia restaurant, and the computer. This

Ferranti 'Argus' computer is programmed to process all data logging, alarm scanning, machinery control, weather forecasting, and the control of all items of stock carried aboard the ship. It is also used to predict the amount of fresh water needed. This is distilled from sea water by three low-pressure evaporators which can produce up to 1,200 tons a day.

There are 760 hotel staff members. They look

after the 564 de luxe and 1441 standard class passengers on the North Atlantic run, or 1350 one-class passengers on a cruise, who occupy 291 de luxe and 687 standard class rooms and 30 public rooms. This highly trained staff ensure that all who sail in the world's finest and most modern ship enjoy the supremely high standards of cuisine, comfort and service for which Cunard have been famous for 130 years.

13

When QE2 was launched there were 760 hotel staff members looking after 564 First Class and 1,441 Tourist Class passengers. Today QE2 has just over a thousand crew members, most of whom are engaged in looking after the comfort and requirements of up to 1,854 passengers. The longest-serving four-stripe officer in the history of the Atlantic 'Queens', John Duffy, is Hotel Manager, responsible for co-ordinating all passenger operations. *Cunard Archives, New York*

On 19 November 1969 QE2 made her first voyage at a steady 7 knots along the 13 miles of the Clyde from the fitting-out basin to the Greenock dry dock. Prince Charles was on the Bridge with the Master, Commodore William E. Warwick. A week later the liner went on sea trials, while workmen continued fitting out her interior. Following a fault in the high-pressure steam system she returned to dry dock. After Christmas 1969 speed trials were resumed and QE2 reached a speed of 32.46 knots along the measured 'Admiralty Mile' off the coast of the Isle of Arran. This photograph shows her wonderful descending series of aft decks - such an expanse of open deck has never been equalled. *Cunard Archives, New York*

Left Commodore William E. Warwick, the first Master of QE2 reads about his beloved ship during the 25th anniversary voyage from Southampton to New York on 8th May 1994. Also on that crossing was the original maiden voyage cabaret star from 25 years ago - Edmund Hockridge. Commodore Warwick is pictured on board QE2 in front of an impressive canvas of the Mauretania departing from the River Tyne, where she was built. This fine painting by T. Henry now hangs on Quarter Deck, starboard side, forward of the Chart Room and is part of the Heritage Trail. *Alan Chandler*

Introduction

No other modern cruise ship can compare with *Queen Elizabeth 2*; indeed, no passenger ship in the history of crossing and cruising can boast such a litany of superlatives as QE2 - the flagship of Britain's Merchant Marine.

In 31 memorable years, Cunard's *Queen Mary* amassed her own amazing record - 1,001 transatlantic crossings, conveying more than three million passengers. QE2 celebrated her magnificent millennium - 1,000 voyages - on a crossing from New York to Southampton on 14 June 1995. The world's last superliner has travelled over 3,900,000 nautical miles, carried 1.75 million passengers in not inconsiderable luxury, and is only 26 years young.

Queen Elizabeth 2 represents one of the most complex integrations of design and machinery ever attempted by man - a vessel capable of going almost anywhere on the globe covered by oceans, with nearly 2,000 passengers and 1,000 crew at a speed in excess of 30 miles per hour in the height of luxury.

When Cunard accepted their new 'Queen of the Seas' on 20 April 1969, the price tag was £29,091,000. Since then Cunard has spent six times as much on refurbishment and renewal! No other vessel has ever had so much money spent on her. No other ship has been transformed so much during such an illustrious career!

'More Carlton Tower than Savoy, brassy rather than serene,' was one description of QE2 following her maiden voyage. *The Times* reported: 'The impression is of good 1960s hotel design compared with good 1930s design of the old Queens. Moulded wood, wrought metal, folk-weave, and damask are out; plastic, tweed, leather are in.' The *Daily Telegraph* wrote: 'There's nothing of the old lady about the new *Queen Elizabeth 2*. She is smart, crisp and modern, using new colours and fabrics and materials.' Informed observers truly believed that in 1969 the new Cunarder was 25 years ahead of her time. From Norman Hartnell's 'turtle-neck' outfits for the waiters and more than two million square feet of brightly-coloured Formica, to today's white-gloved service and rich fabrics in regal hues, QE2 has always been at the forefront of fashion, offering a taste of the high life on the high seas.

QE2 emerged from the trendy Swinging Sixties, survived the economic shockwave of the Seventies and sailed through the enlightened Eighties to come of age in 1988. With new motive power, she emerged full of youth and vitality to sail with renewed vigour into the exciting Nineties. With creative designs incorporated during the 1994 refit, this gracious dowager duchess is in the prime of her life as she sails towards the next millennium - vast, confident and wonderfully stately.

In 1987 QE2 underwent the greatest marine engineering conversion ever, giving her a new heart in the form of diesel-electric propulsion. In 1994 it was her body that was recreated, offering a halcyon hideaway on the high seas. As for her soul - passengers and crew certainly agree that QE2 is truly a joyous vestige of a great maritime tradition.

Passengers have a preoccupation with QE2, partly because she is a conduit to rekindling memories of a lost era - a brief glimpse into the remarkable world in which their forefathers crossed oceans in the grand days of travel, and partly because the best things happen at sea.

Old traditions do not necessarily mean old ships. QE2 offers satellite newspapers delivered daily to your cabin in a variety of languages, a computer learning centre and a thalassotherapy centre. There are also plenty of opportunities to relive the high life on the ocean swells. Glamorous ladies in ball gowns and men sporting tuxedos with a brandy in hand are all part of

Before and after In December 1983, during QE2's annual refit, the Bremerhaven yard fitted a Magrodome glass roof over the Quarter Deck swimming pool, making it available for use in all weathers. This retractable glass canopy was removed in the 1994 refit - as was the Quarter Deck swimming pool itself. Also during the 1983 refit, two 45-foot cruise tenders were added aft on Boat Deck. They could carry 118 passengers and assisted in ship-to-shore tender operations. The complicated supports for Alpha and Beta disrupted the flow of the open decks aft and were also removed in the 1994 refit. QE2 now has a much cleaner open-deck profile, which is proving very popular with passengers during fine weather cruising. *Cunard, London*

life's rich tapestry on board QE2. Guests enjoy evoking a period when time was not so precious, when crossing the Atlantic was measured in days, not hours, before grace gave way to pace, and when the journey, not the destination, was the important thing. After all, to paraphrase a famous Cunard poster, getting there is half the fun.

The promotional brochure for QE2 in 1969 reflects how little this pleasure island has changed. The flagship of the Cunard Line was revolutionary, boasting the most extensive facilities of any ship afloat. In 'Ships have been boring long enough', Cunard highlighted these unique features:

'The QE2 is a resort in her own right, self-contained and self-sufficient. She distils her own fresh water from the sea, she has her own shops and banks, her own systems of communication and she launders all her own linen. Indeed, within her thirteen decks she provides all the amenities of a small, immaculately appointed town. There's a complete valeting service for pressing and dry cleaning - and naturally a laundry. But if you would rather do your own washing, there are three launderettes for passengers, complete with automatic washing machines, irons and ironing boards. Hairdressing is often the last consideration in drawing up the layout of a ship, and is fitted into whatever space is left over. Here it was planned on an opulent scale from the start. The women's salon, like the men's barber shop, is run by Steiner. To give you some idea of its spaciousness, it has twelve setting positions and 16 dryers as well as its separate beauty treatment room. On the Boat Deck is a shopping arcade with stores selling duty-free perfume and cosmetics; clothes, and in particular English and Scottish knitwear; gifts in china and glass and other fancy goods; and jewellery. And below is an exclusive shop where even finer things are displayed. Alongside the shopping arcade the picture gallery, run by the Marlborough Art Galleries of New Bond Street, will keep an exhibition of paintings, drawings, sculpture and objets d'art. The QE2 has its own photographic studio whose cameramen attend every function and party. To care for babies, there's a crèche near the children's play area in the charge of a nursery stewardess. And even pets are made to feel important; dogs have their own special kennels with a view of the sea and their special exercise area. One service you hope you will not require - although it is reassuring to know it's there - is the hospital, which has a fully equipped operating theatre, X-ray and physiotherapy rooms and a dental surgery. While for most people an ocean voyage is a complete holiday, some passengers like to work their passage. For them the ship can provide, apart from peace and quiet, a complete secretarial and translation service, and the use of typewriters and Dictaphones. And any printing can be quickly done on the ship's presses. Business groups can book the theatre by day for their meetings. It has been designed for that purpose. There are even facilities for simultaneous translation, with soundproof glass booths for the interpreters and earphones for the delegates. Smaller conference rooms are also available. But if QE2 gives you privacy for thinking, it doesn't make you feel cut off. The ship's newspaper and radio telephone keep you in touch with the world. The market prices come over the wire. Cunard had business executives very much in mind when they thought of all the services that their *new ship* should provide.'

The locations may have changed, there are more grill rooms and the radio telephone is now operated by satellite, but with the exception of some minor changes and many additions, including the largest passenger library afloat, florist and spa, QE2 still offers passengers the ultimate floating resort.

'There's no hotel or restaurant in the world,' said Jimmy Smith, the first Hotel Manager of the QE2 back in 1969, 'where you'll find a higher standard of food and of presentation than aboard this ship.' One thousand voyages later this sentiment is echoed by the present Hotel Manager, John Duffy, who has been instrumental in keeping QE2 at the forefront of epicurean trends to ensure that the whims and caprices of all passengers on board this city at sea are satisfied.

This recent view of QE2 shows her restored open decks aft of the mighty funnel. Forward of the funnel can be seen the penthouse suites, which were added successively in the 1972 annual refit at Vosper Thorneycroft in Southampton, the 1977 annual refit at the Bethlehem Steel Shipyard in Bayonne, New Jersey, and finally eight more were added during the major 1987 refit at Lloyd Werft in Bremerhaven. The attractive 'speed stripe' just below Quarter Deck was added during the 1994 Blohm & Voss refit in Hamburg. *Alan Chandler*

Fares in 1969 for a one-way transatlantic crossing ranged from $255 Tourist Class in the thrift season to $542 in the summer season. Today fares range from $1,495 in super value season to $10,450 in peak season. The greater differential in these fares between minimum and top grades reflects the addition and upgrading of the luxury cabins and suites since the ship was commissioned.

The various changes to both public rooms and passenger accommodations are detailed in the forthcoming pages. Refit by refit, the metamorphosis of *Queen Elizabeth 2* is reflected in archive and contemporary photographs. No reader could fail to be impressed at the continual fresh face the great Cunarder has sported at so many stages throughout her most illustrious career. For those seeking a wealth of historic information as well as anecdotal highlights about QE2, Captain Ronald Warwick's book *QE2 - The Cunard Line Flagship*, 2nd edition, published by W. W. Norton, could not be more highly recommended.

QE2 is truly the Queen of the Seas, but the relationship between Her Majesty Queen Elizabeth II and the Cunard vessel requires some clarification. When Her Majesty Queen Elizabeth II launched the vessel one sunny afternoon in September 1967, she spoke these words: 'I name this ship Queen Elizabeth the Second. May God Bless her and all who sail in her.' This immediately began one of the biggest maritime puzzles. Surely this must have been the only occasion in history when a shipping company had to try to explain what the name of the ship meant. Did it refer to Her Majesty, Queen Elizabeth the Second (it will be recalled that the original liner was named after the Queen Consort of King George VI)? Or was the name meant to imply the second *Queen Elizabeth* liner? The riddle was solved by the Cunard Chairman of the day, Sir Basil Smallpeice. 'The liner is named after the monarch, but I do not feel we should use "Queen Elizabeth II", which is the official designation of the Queen as Sovereign. I thought the use of an Arabic 2, instead of a Roman II, might make a sufficient distinction, and I was pleased to hear from Lord Adeane, the Queen's Private Secretary, that Her Majesty had approved the styling of the ship as "Queen Elizabeth 2".'

Captain Ronald W. Warwick has, in his personal collection, confirmation from Buckingham Palace that the liner is indeed named after the Monarch - but in the style of an Arabic 2. To this day passengers and even some writers incorrectly employ the sovereign's roman numeral rather than the ship's Arabic one. So any reference to Queen Elizabeth II is to the monarch, not the Cunard vessel that bears her name. In 1969 Assistant Purser Harry Smith received a letter addressed to 'The QE II'. He promptly marked it 'Try Buckingham Palace' and returned it to the Post Office.

'Ship-shape and in Cunard fashion' is an appropriate epithet for this regal ship - the last in that great lineage of ocean-going liners. Today, as she matures like a fine wine, QE2 is setting an historic course into the next millennium.

CUNARD

On 7 May 1969 QE2 makes her maiden arrival into New York harbour. The accompanying flotilla exchanged salutes as the new transatlantic 'Queen' completed her first crossing in 4 days, 16 hours and 35 minutes, at an average speed of 28.02 knots. Note the skyline of Lower Manhattan and Battery Park from the Hudson River. *Collection R. W. Warwick*

Right A quarter of a century on, the profile of QE2 has changed little in comparison with the New York skyline. During an arrival the ship lists gently to port, while on departure from New York the list is to starboard as passengers catch a glimpse of Lady Liberty - symbol of hope for so many in years gone by. *Alan Chandler*

Right in the centre of Manhattan at the Passenger Ship Terminal at 55th Street - better known by many as Pier 90 - QE2 prepares to sail from Berth 3. The well-rehearsed departure sequence begins: the various victualling ramps are withdrawn and soon the only remaining link between the ship and pier is the passenger gangway. Soon that too is landed as tugs take up position. QE2 gives three long blasts on her deep whistle (an 'A' - four octaves below Middle 'A'). On board, passengers experience a slight vibration as the mighty diesel-electric engines begin to turn the propeller shafts. Up to 1,854 passengers set off as the greatest hotel afloat leaves town. *Ocean Pictures*

A Southampton departure may not enjoy such a dramatic backdrop, but the event is no less memorable. A brass band plays 'Sailing' then 'Rule Britannia', followed by 'Auld Lang Syne', bringing a lump to the throat, if not a tear to the eye, of the waving passengers lining the Boat Deck as QE2 heads seaward from the recently refurbished Queen Elizabeth II Terminal at Southampton. *Alan Chandler*

Above During QE2's annual visit to Sydney as part of her World Cruise itinerary, Circular Quay buzzes with excitement. Any sail away from Sydney is always a tumultuous event with the scenic harbour festooned with small craft bidding a farewell to the mighty Cunarder. Curiously, QE2 did not visit Sydney as part of her first World Cruise in 1975 - it was not until February 1978 that this majestic harbour first welcomed this magnificent ship. Since then, Sydney has featured in every World Cruise itinerary. *Alan Chandler*

Left Sunset as QE2 sets sail from Taiwan as part of her 1995 Golden Route World Cruise. The Sports Deck observation area just below the Bridge is always a popular vantage point. Just below the port-side crane can be seen the container that serves as a crew swimming pool during the World Cruise. Deck officers and hands ensure that the fo'c'sle is ship-shape and in Cunard fashion. The winching gear for the two forward anchors is clearly visible. Each anchor weighs 12.5 tons and is attached to a 1,080-foot cable whose massive links are each 4 inches in diameter. *Alan Chandler*

QE2 experiences all types of weather. During the World Cruise she follows the sun, but during her December transatlantic crossings the weather can sometimes be less than friendly. In 1985 One Deck Lido was snow-covered as this view from Quarter Deck shows. *Ocean Pictures*

The unforgiving North Atlantic is a force to be reckoned with. Nothing teaches lay mariners a greater respect for the sea than experiencing a transatlantic crossing in a Force 9 or above. This view, taken in May 1995, reflects the strength of QE2's hull - no other cruise ship could withstand such conditions without suffering serious structural damage - or worse.

Four months later, on the night of 10 September 1995, QE2 encountered Hurricane Luis. Winds in excess of Force 12 were recorded - at one point 130 miles per hour. The average wave height was 40 feet with one specific wave at 90 feet. Captain Warwick reduced the ship's speed to 5 knots. *Ocean Pictures*

QE2's annual visit to the North Cape is one of her most popular cruises. This view, taken at 12.30 am in July 1995, shows a serene QE2 at anchor off Skarsvaag - latitude 71 degrees North. The Land of the Midnight Sun must surely be one of the most remote destinations in QE2's annual cruising schedule. *Rocky Page*

Left The original Bridge of QE2. Since 1969 no fewer than 17 Captains have taken command of Britain's merchant marine flagship, of which nine were appointed Captains. Commodore William E. Warwick was the first Master of QE2, and today his son, Captain Ronald W. Warwick, regularly follows in his father's footsteps as Captain. There is only one occasion when the Captain relinquishes command of his ship; during QE2's annual transit of the Panama Canal regulations dictate that the senior pilot assigned to the vessel has control of the navigation and movement of QE2 - although naturally he always consults the Master. *Brian Price*

Below left The Bridge of QE2 today. In this oasis of calm efficiency the officers of the watch use some of the most advanced maritime technology available. The Bridge is linked with all the operating areas, including the Safety Control Room, and is provided with remote control of the electro-hydraulic doors throughout the vessel. *Gary Buchanan*

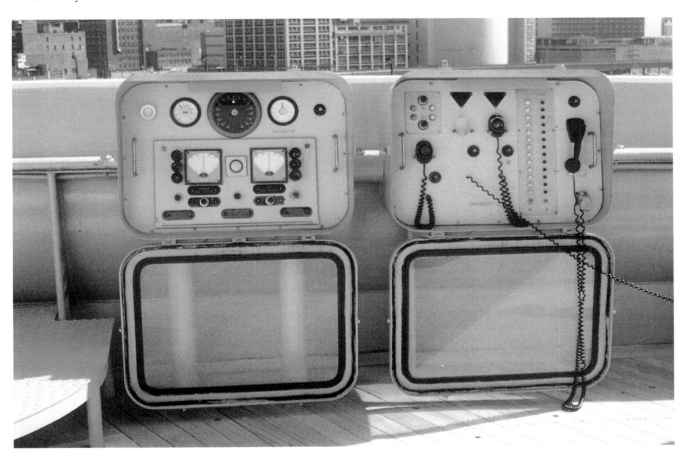

Above These original Bridge Wing controls have now been superseded by a modern panel that allows the Captain greater flexibility to control the rudder and the speed of the ship as well as the bow thrusters. *Brian Price*

Navigational equipment is now completely computerised. There are now three state-of-the-art Kelvin Hughes radars (not shown) affording both daylight and night-time viewing, with a computerised facility for plotting targets automatically. There are Decca and Loran navigators, a Marconi direction finder for coastal position fixing, and a Magnavox Satellite Omega Navigator and Global Positioning System for ocean passages. The Magnavox is linked directly to channel 19 on the televisions of each passenger cabin. This gives the ship's position (affording much amusement when QE2 crosses the equator or Greenwich Meridian) as well as the ship's course and speed.
Gary Buchanan

The original Chart Room of QE2, which is still in use today, lies aft of the Bridge. It contains up-to-date charts of all the major, and many minor, coastlines and waterways of the world. *Brian Price*

Above The Main Control Room is the principal watchkeeping station in the machinery spaces. *Brian Price*

Below The Turbine Control Room and the Main Control Room monitored under remote control, allowed the Chief Engineer and his team to keep a constant watch of all aspects associated with the complete running of the main power plant. When launched, QE2 had the most sophisticated and advanced computer installation ever used in a merchant ship - 'ARGUS'. *Brian Price*

Above The Engine Control Room today. Data from the diesel electric engines and ancillary services is fed electronically to this comfortable control room, which allows the engineering officers to monitor all aspects of the ship's propulsion, generating and distribution systems. Closed-circuit television cameras provide a constant visual surveillance of the machinery in 26 locations. The entrance is on Seven Deck and, like the other mechanical areas of QE2, is off-limits to even the most curious passengers. *Gary Buchanan*

Below The Safety Control Room, located amidships on Two Deck, has changed little over 26 years. Here, master plans of the ship showing all the safety features are on display, as this early view shows. There are also controls indicating the amount of fuel, fresh water and ballast water contained in all the tanks. *Brian Price*

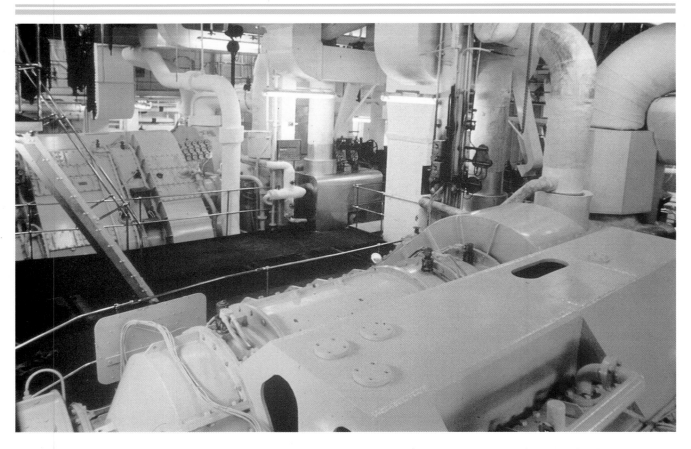

Above left The three turbine generators, manufactured by AEI and installed in QE2 during construction, were each capable of producing a maximum of 5,500kW of electrical power at 3,300 volts at 60Hz and were the largest turbine generators ever built for ship-board use. This fine view shows the Main Engine Room when QE2 was launched. The two main engine gear boxes gave a maximum installed power of 110,000 shaft horsepower through dual tandem reduction gears of John Brown-Pametrada design. The three JBE-Foster Wheeler boilers each weighed up to 278 tons and were the largest ever to be used in a ship. The steam turbines, boilers and gears successfully propelled QE2 over two million nautical miles. *Brian Price*

Left This dramatic view was taken during the re-engining of QE2 at the £180 million refit at Lloyd Werft in Bremerhaven, which lasted 179 days from 27 October 1986 until 25 April 1987, and was a task of leviathan proportions. The cavernous Engine Room is seen with 4,700 tons of steam propulsion equipment removed. The first of nine diesel generators - dubbed Alpha - rests in place in the forward port-side corner of the empty, cathedral-like Engine Room. *Lloyd Werft*

Above Today QE2 is fitted with nine medium-speed diesel engines, each weighing 217 tons and with an output of 10,620kW (14,236 hp) at 400 revolutions per minute. They are arranged athwartships in two groups: four in the forward Engine Room and five in the after Engine Room. Each diesel engine is connected with a flexible coupling to an alternator to produce electricity. The power from all nine generators is fed directly to a common 10kV busbar system, divided into two separate switchboards. The propulsion motors, made by GEC Large Machines Ltd, are believed to be the largest single-unit propulsion motors in commercial service. Each weighs 295 tons and is rated at 44 MW synchronous running at 144 rpm; they have a diameter of about 30 feet. Each motor is connected to a 230-foot-long propeller shaft inclined downwards at 1.5 degrees to the horizontal, extending sternward to each side of the rudder. *Alan Chandler*

The Queen's Room on Quarter Deck, designed by Michael Inchbald in 1969, had a sense of spaciousness as well as a lengthened fore and aft look with a sunny, garden-like atmosphere. The white shell chairs on trumpet-shaped bases echoed in reverse the white fibre-glass structural columns. White lacquered sofas with 150 scatter cushions made up in three colours - pale orange, yellow and beige - complemented the shell chairs' fabric of natural hide. Fine wool curtains dressed the sliding glass walls between this room and the Quarter Deck promenades. *William H. Miller*

This beautiful room was QE2's answer to the Grand Salon of the great 'Queens'. The slotted white ceiling with rear lighting gave a trellised effect as this night-time view shows. The soft elegance and muted lighting, even today, create the perfect atmosphere for an elegant Captain's welcome party or an evening of dancing. *Cunard Archives, New York*

Cubic armchairs in soft brown leather replaced the shell chairs during the 1987 refit. The Queen's Room is the focal hub of the ship every afternoon as that great British tradition, afternoon tea, becomes a daily ritual. In the morning, dance and yoga classes are held, emphasising the versatility of this most splendid room. *Cunard Archives, London*

The Queen's Room was once again treated to a facelift during the 1994 refit; it is now adorned with comfortable chairs in mustard yellow and deep royal blue. A magnificent new focal point has been created, centred on the bronze bust of Her Majesty Queen Elizabeth II. This regal sculpture by Oscar Nemon is now framed against a velvet background in a central spot-lit alcove, backlit in an impressive deep blue. *Ocean Pictures*

Probably the most dramatic of the public rooms on board QE2 was the Double Room, seen here in 1969. Two decks high, the Double Up Room and Bar on Boat Deck were linked to the Upper Deck dance floor, Double Down Room and Aft Bar by a stainless steel spiral staircase with a glass balustrade and red hand-rails. The Double Room, designed by Jon Bannenberg, covered a vast 20,000 square feet and seated 800 passengers. The spiral staircase led not on to the dance floor but into the Double Down Bar, and there is an apocryphal story that this grand spiral staircase was fitted the wrong way round. *Cunard Archives, New York*

Looking forward from the Boat Deck level of the Double Room, the large dance floor and bandstand give a wonderful impression of space. When visitors first toured QE2 in New York in May 1969, they were astonished to learn that this was the main lounge for Tourist Class passengers. (QE2 was originally designed to accommodate First, Tourist and Third Class passengers on line voyages. By the time QE2 was launched Cunard had opted for a two-class ship. Today in the egalitarian 1990s she offers both First and Transatlantic Classes on crossings, while on cruises QE2 is all one class - with subtle differentiation between Grill, Caronia and Mauretania grade cabins. *Cunard Archives, New York*

Following the 1987 refit, the spiral staircase at the aft end of the Double Room was removed and a very elegant twin staircase created on each side of the stage at the forward end of the room - then renamed the Grand Lounge. The sound and light system was controlled from a production booth at the rear balcony on Boat Deck. The International Shopping Promenade, stretching down either side of Boat Deck on the upper level of the Grand Lounge, was modernised from its utilitarian design created during the 1987 refit. *Cunard Archives, New York*

The 1994 refit brought further changes. The delightful twin spiral staircase was removed in favour of a much larger thrust stage, and the dance floor was removed. Modern production shows require a considerable stage area, not to mention dressing rooms. This dedicated show lounge now accommodates almost 700 passengers and is regularly packed to capacity with glitzy production shows, top-billing entertainers, and something that has proved to be a recent great success - a crew show - to a packed house of delighted passengers. *Alan Chandler*

Above The Q 4 Room took its name from the popular title ascribed to QE2 before she was christened. Designed by David Hicks, this First Class hideaway night club doubled by day as the lounge bar for the Quarter Deck Lido. It was a coolly professional room that proved to be very popular with the late-night set; indeed, late-night meals were available. Black tweed banquettes, black and grey tablecloths and wall panels of grey flannel encased in aluminium frames were set off by a carpet of black, grey and red checks. Translucent screens made of perspex rods sandwiched between sheets of polarised glass produced a rainbow effect of soft colours, enhancing the sophisticated tone of this room. *Cunard Archives, New York*

Below The Q 4 Room was replaced by the Club Lido during the 1983 refit at Lloyd Werft in Bremerhaven. The bar that served both the Q 4 Room and the Quarter Deck Lido was repositioned to the centre of the room on the port side, and a glass dance floor and adjacent bandstand added. At this time the Magrodome was fitted over the pool and deck area; this retractable glass roof created a complete indoor and outdoor entertainment and leisure area. This remained the late-night spot on QE2 until the total transformation of the whole area into the Lido Cafe at the 1994 refit at Blohm & Voss in Hamburg. *Collection R. W. Warwick*

Right The Yacht Club replaced the Double Down Aft Bar in 1987. The nautical decor, with a wave-shaped ceiling, featured pictures and models of yachts that had participated in America's Cup races. The glass-enclosed piano proved popular with a regular night-time clientele, while the whole bar attracted a discerning mix of passengers who enjoyed the intimacy and conviviality. *Cunard Archives, London*

Right Drastically redesigned in the 1994 refit, the Yacht Club today sports a quarter-moon-shaped bar, together with a distinguished colour scheme. The disco-nightclub, complete with live band, is now the late-night haunt on board. With windows aft, to port and starboard, in inclement weather it is an excellent vantage point from which to watch QE2 arrive and depart from ports. The nautical theme has been continued with half hulls of America's Cup yachts displayed on the forward, wooden wall. *Niall Clutton/MET Studio Ltd, London*

Above The Theatre Bar, originally designed by Dennis Lennon and adjacent to the Theatre on Upper Deck, starboard side, sported Victorian chairs in red tweed along with big chunky settees in red, while the back of the bar looked like an egg crate in brilliant red fibre-glass. This was a popular social venue for pre-dinner cocktails as well as the Tourist Class nightclub.

The interior was changed in the 1972 refit, making the appearance very stark by today's standards, but considered ultra-modern at the time. As can be seen, red was the predominant colour for the Theatre Bar until it was changed in the 1987 refit, when low-slung, blue leather chairs toned down the colour scheme of this lively spot. *Collection Peter Boyd-Smith at Cobwebs*

Left In the 1994 refit the Theatre Bar became the Golden Lion Pub, taking its name from the famous golden Cunard symbol of an amiable crowned lion rearing up on its hindquarters and facing forwards as if seeking approval after having retrieved a ball. Today this latter-day interpretation of a Victorian-style pub serves a wide variety of beers and is still a popular pre-lunch or dinner meeting point. Aft of the Golden Lion is the photographic display area of Ocean Pictures - a Southampton-based company that has been photographing life on the high seas since the concept began. *Niall Clutton/MET Studio Ltd, London*

The Observation Bar, created by Theo Crosby, was the only forward-facing public room on QE2. Also known as the Lookout Bar, this popular room, on Upper Deck forward, was panelled in cedar veneer with chairs and stools in black leather. The floor was carpeted in dark green and a red plastic chart reader was positioned by the windows, giving the ship's position. Sadly, 1972 saw the demise of this room as space was at a premium for a new dedicated galley following the transformation and increase in capacity of the Britannia Restaurant. In 1977 the name of this restaurant was changed to Tables of the World. The white box-like structure above the fo'c'sle, below the Bridge, also houses part of the galley of what is now the Caronia Restaurant. *Cunard Archives, New York*

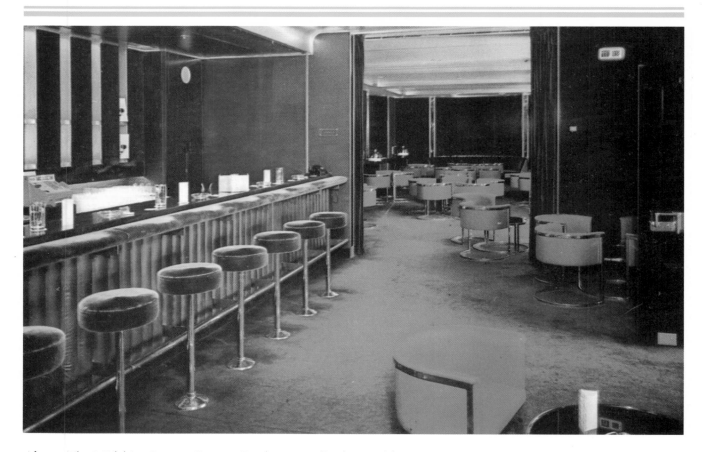

Above The Midships Bar on Quarter Deck, originally designed by Dennis Lennon, was themed as a dark, intimate room with little touches of brightness from enamels and brass. The chairs were in bright emerald-green mohair and velvet and the onion-shaped lights in polished brass sparkled low over the rosewood tables to help create this intimate atmosphere. *Collection Peter Boyd-Smith at Cobwebs*

Left Remaining relatively unchanged from its original appearance, 25 years on the Midships Bar was transformed into the Chart Room during the 1994 refit. The room now sports clean lines, but has lost a degree of intimacy. The Chart Room lives up to its new maritime theme by sporting a glass-topped antique burr-walnut chest containing present-day navigational charts; there is also a display of antique nautical instruments. A specially commissioned calligraphic frieze by Brody Neuenschwander comprises quotations from various illustrious characters who have sailed the Atlantic. Each evening passengers in the Chart Room are entertained with melodies played on the magnificent maple grand piano that originally graced the Queen Mary *Niall Clutton/MET Studio Ltd, London*

Above The large picture windows afford unobstructed views of the sea, while just forward of this room is another favourite focal point - the many-thousand-piece jigsaw. *Niall Clutton/MET Studio Ltd, London*

Right A tradition of the great Atlantic 'Queens' has been recreated behind the Chart Room Bar. The glass panel depicts the north Atlantic and the Great Circle Route taken by QE2 during her many transatlantic crossings - up to 30 each year. A similar, but more elegant, glass map designed by Macdonald Gill can still be seen in the Cabin Class Restaurant on board the *Queen Mary* in her adopted new home of Long Beach, California. *Niall Clutton/MET Studio Ltd, London*

Above The Crystal Bar was created in the 1994 refit. This large room, stretching the entire width of the ship, forward on Upper Deck, now gives passengers dining in the Caronia Restaurant, as well as the Britannia and Princess Grills, a convenient social meeting point. The Art Deco-style semi-circular wooden bar features a reproduction glass bas-relief of 'Winged Horse and Clouds', similar to that which graced the *Queen Elizabeth*. *Niall Clutton/MET Studio Ltd, London*

Above right When QE2 was launched, the One Deck Shop, amidships by D stairway, sold very exclusive jewellery. During the 1972 refit the shop was moved to the existing shopping arcade on Boat Deck, between D and E stairways - when that too was located aft of the E stairway. The One Deck room was converted at that time into a bar known as Club Atlantic. *Cunard Archives, New York*

Right When the liner *France* ended her North Atlantic service, staff members from the French ship were employed on board QE2 to work in the Club Atlantic. Service was distinguished and waiters spoke five different languages. Sadly, Cunard's tribute to the *France* was short-lived. Despite this elegant bar attracting discerning passengers, it was subsequently closed and the area reverted to a shop specialising in china and crystal. During the 1984 refit, the first - and only - ocean-going branch of Harrods opened in this central location. *Cunard Archives, New York*

Above An early view of Queen's Grill Lounge on Boat Deck, starboard side. Originally this room was the Coffee Shop and had changed its function several times even before the ship was commissioned. Cunard planned to use this space as a bowling alley, but by the time QE2 sailed on her maiden voyage this long room, with unimpeded views out on to the promenade area of Boat Deck, had become a 24-hour Coffee Shop and Teenage Juke Box Room. Waitress service was available to passengers wishing light snacks or even a breakfast in the small hours, while in the area of the Juke Box Room, there were pinball machines, a juke box and distorting mirrors. This concept only lasted for three years, when the room was converted into the Queen's Grill Lounge during the 1972 refit. *Cunard Archives, New York*

Right The Queen's Grill Lounge has sported a number of interior decors. In 1982 it was remodelled, along with the Queen's Grill, by Dennis Lennon. Following the 1994 refit the room is now an elegant retreat, sporting some fine original paintings on the inside wall. The soft furnishings were changed and large, comfortable midnight-blue armchairs added. In the forward, smoking section of the lounge, adjacent to the small bar, regular Queen's Grill passengers take up their usual positions either at their favourite table, close by the large picture window, or at their familiar bar stool. *Niall Clutton/McNeece Ltd, London*

THE LIBRARY
GUILDFORD COLLEGE
of Further and Higher Education

Above Amongst the most successful and sophisticated rooms on the *Queen Elizabeth* and *Queen Mary* were the Verandah Grills. When QE2 was launched, she too had an exclusive restaurant that was available to all First Class passengers on payment of a supplement of 10 shillings (50p, or 75c - today). The Grill Room was located forward of the Columbia Restaurant on Quarter Deck, although access was via a steel spiral staircase that led up from the small, intimate Grill Room Bar on One Deck. Dennis Lennon aimed to create a sophisticated, rich atmosphere with plum velvet panelling on the walls and matching plum leather chairs with touches of chromium. The ribbed ceiling in silver aluminium reflected the oyster-coloured silk curtains and pink tablecloths. The central area had, at each corner, four statues by Janine Janet representing the Four Elements. Illuminated and standing about 5 feet high, they were constructed entirely of marine items, such as mother-of-pearl, coral and shells. These four statues grace the Princess Grill to this day. *Cunard Archives, New York*

Left The Princess Grill, probably more than any other room on board QE2, remains the same today as it did when discerning passengers first compared Cunard's new approach to luxury with the famous Atlantic 'Queens' back in 1969. The name changed with the advent of the Queen's Grill, while the entrance was altered in the 1994 refit and passengers now descend from the Crystal Bar on Upper Deck to this delightful sanctuary in pink and burgundy. Seating just 100 guests, this sophisticated grill room enjoys magnificent sea views and as such has remained a firm favourite amongst many repeat passengers. *Niall Clutton/MET Studio Ltd, London*

Right When QE2 was commissioned, the 736 Club occupied the room that is now the Queen's Grill. '736' was the building number assigned to QE2 by John Brown's prior to her naming ceremony in the Clyde on 20 September 1967. Designed by Stefan Buzas, the 736 Club was a bar by day and a club by night. One evening a rather famous drummer decided to relieve the resident percussionist - Ringo Starr entertained the club's patrons accompanying the band in several Beatles hit songs. After a few months this room briefly became Juliana's Discotheque before being transformed into the Casino. QE2 did not have a casino when she entered service due to restrictive laws that existed in the United States. When the laws were relaxed, this handsome room, forward on Boat Deck, became the Casino for a brief period before that too was finally relocated to Upper Deck, port side.

When the first penthouses were added in the 1972 refit at Vosper Thorneycroft, this spacious room became the most exclusive restaurant on board. Restaurant and grill rooms were allocated depending on stateroom category and passengers in the luxury suites on Signal and Sports Decks as well as the deluxe cabins and suites on One and Two Decks dined in the Queen's Grill. This same arrangement exists today. The Queen's Grill was further extended forward on the starboard side with the addition of eight more penthouse suites in 1986. *Niall Clutton/MET Studio Ltd, London*

Below Today this exclusive grill room accommodates 240 passengers who enjoy cuisine prepared in a dedicated small galley just aft of the Grill. The gold leaf ceiling of the lower, central section still reflects the flambé dishes, while the off-white leather chairs and black velour banquets were replaced in the 1994 refit. Individual white leather chairs give a distinguished feel to this room, which represents the epitome of service on the high seas. Crowning the room, on the aft bulkhead, is the Royal Coat of Arms in polished wood. Unlike the Princess Grill, probably no other room on QE2 has been transformed as much as the Queen's Grill. *Terry Yarwood*

Above left The Columbia Restaurant on Quarter Deck, designed by Dennis Lennon, had a subtle, sophisticated air with mink brown leather panels at each end of the room that complemented a pale brown carpet mirrored by a silver ceiling in ribbed aluminium. The curtains were in pale apricot with off-white blinds to stop the glare from the big windows, and between some of the tables were tinted glass screens. The chairs, in dark brown leather, showed up the pale lemon tablecloths at breakfast and lunch, while at dinner the motif changed to pink. There was a small dance floor, while down the centre of the room were louvres of aluminium and tinted perspex. Lennon described the room as 'not a dominating room, it is a room which provides a background for people'. It seated 500 guests. *Cunard Archives, New York*

Left Subtle changes were made to the Columbia Restaurant throughout QE2's early life. The chairs changed from dark brown to cream and finally, in the 1987 refit, to pink velour. The tablecloths remained as pale pink while the pyramid table lights were replaced with dainty night-lights. Throughout the first 25 years of QE2's illustrious career the focal point of the small, elegant staircase into the Columbia Restaurant was the silver vase given to Samuel Cunard by the citizens of Boston. This was to celebrate the first regular steamship service carrying mails and passengers across the Atlantic by the wooden-hulled paddle-steamer *Britannia* in July 1840. The intricate silver urn is now part of the Samuel Cunard Collection on the Heritage Trail at the Yacht Club Lobby on Upper Deck. *Cunard Archives, London*

Above The most dramatic change occurred during the 1994 refit when the Columbia Restaurant became the Mauretania Restaurant. The colour scheme was changed to dark cream chairs, white tablecloths and a Cunard Golden Lion-emblazoned maroon and gold carpet. A large model of the *Mauretania* is the centrepiece of the room, but the massive illuminated model of that ship aft of the entrance is truly impressive. The gargantuan galley has a small separate kitchen that serves the Princess and Britannia Grills. *Alan Chandler*

The Britannia Restaurant, the largest restaurant on QE2, accommodating 800 passengers, was also designed by Dennis Lennon as a lively room in red, white and blue. Designed to be the Tourist Class restaurant and situated forward on Upper Deck, it had fibre-glass bulkheads that created a tongue-and-groove board effect. The blinds were white with a blue symbol and there were no curtains, while all around the room was a bright red leather handrail. The restaurant was divided into small recesses with duckboard screens, giving it a maritime flavour. The tall windows flooded the room with daylight as the room spanned the entire width of the ship. Tablecloths were white with red borders, while the napkins were red with a white border. The figurehead of Britannia, carved out of Quebec Yellow Pine by Charles Moore, was presented to QE2 by Lloyds of London. This graced the forward entrance on Upper Deck by A stairway, and later the starboard entrance to the Tables of the World Restaurant before being finally moved to its present position at the top of A stairway on Boat Deck.

Originally all food was delivered to the Britannia Restaurant from the main (Columbia) galley one deck below by means of a central pair of escalators. These were removed when the dedicated galley for the Britannia Restaurant was constructed during the 1972 refit. It was at this time that the Lookout Bar ceased to exist, while the name of the restaurant was changed to Tables of the World in 1977. The room was then divided into five different cultural theme sections: Parisian, London, Florentine, Flamenco and Oriental. The dedicated galley considerably improved the efficiency of the service in this restaurant, which operated on a two-seating basis on all voyages except the World Cruise. *Collection Peter Boyd-Smith at Cobwebs*

In the 1987 refit this vast room was changed yet again when the Mauretania Restaurant was created. The decor reverted to a central theme throughout, and warm tones of pink, lilac and purple were introduced. New wall and ceiling panels in Art Deco style were featured, along with many photographs of the original Cunarder. A dance floor under a mirrored ceiling was introduced, giving the room the effect of added height. *Collection R. W. Warwick*

Above The total transformation during the 1994 refit saw the Mauretania Restaurant relocate to Quarter Deck, while the Caronia Restaurant was created in its place. The focal point of this most attractive room is a huge aluminium sculpture depicting 'white horses of the Atlantic ocean' by Althea Wynne. The colour scheme throughout the room is blue and green, set against cream swirls. On the forward bulkhead is a specially commissioned brightly coloured painting by Jane Human of the restaurant's namesake - the Cunarder *Caronia* - in the South Pacific. On the aft wall is a model of the 'Green Goddess' herself - so called because *Caronia* sported no fewer than four shades of green - in addition to a painting by Stephen Card of *Caronia* at Cape Town. *Niall Clutton/MET Studio Ltd, London*

Above right There is a timeless Art Deco quality to this new room, with etched glass panels acting as dividers, thus creating a sense of intimacy in this expansive room. Here in the Caronia Restaurant passengers who have sailed previously on board QE2 can appreciate the continual upgrading that this great vessel has undergone during the course of 1,000 voyages. This reflects Cunard's commitment to improving the quality of the cruising experience on what is surely the world's last dedicated ocean-going liner. *Niall Clutton/MET Studio Ltd, London*

Right Created in the 1990 Hamburg refit from a side room, forward of the Columbia Restaurant on the starboard side, was the Princess Grill Starboard. This room subsequently changed its name to the Britannia Grill, following the changes made in December 1994. Similar in size to the original Princess Grill, in the same location on the port side of the ship, the Britannia Grill has muted tones of mauve and pink. The large windows give a light, airy feel as well as a sense of space. Access to both the Britannia and Princess Grills is by elegant chrome and brass staircases leading down on either side of Upper Deck from the Crystal Bar. *Collection R. W. Warwick*

A large dedicated buffet service area with informal tables and chairs was created in the 1994 refit. The Lido Cafe replaced the Club Lido and Quarter Deck pool, while the Magrodome was removed. This vast room has proved very popular with passengers who enjoy a more casual approach to breakfasts and lunches. It is also a good social gathering point for passengers who have made friends with guests who may be dining in a different restaurant from themselves. This is also the venue for the Midnight Buffet - a sea-going tradition that seems to be less popular in the more health-conscious 1990s. There are two self-service buffet lines in addition to a central self-service island buffet. The large windows to port, starboard and aft - overlooking the One Deck pool - make this casual dining option rather pleasant during warm weather cruising. *Alan Chandler*

One deck below and linked to the Lido Cafe by a pair of staircases is the Pavilion. Looking out on to One Deck with its large swimming pool, this new self-service, call-order grill serves hamburgers, hot dogs and steak sandwiches. A casual room, light and airy and complete with a bar serving the pool area, it has replaced the rather impractical, not to mention run-down, 'Hamburger Haven' and open pool bar. *Gary Buchanan*

Above The Quarter Deck pool in 1969 - note the wonderful open teak decking. When the Magrodome was added, tables and chairs surrounded the enclosed pool area and the deck was covered in green Astroturf. The pool was removed in 1994 and the whole area roofed over to become the Lido Cafe. Designed by James Gardner, this pool, aft of the Q 4 Room, had a canopy above its forward end, which was heated from above so that warmth could be enjoyed by bathers on cooler days; on transatlantic voyages and early cruises this was the First Class pool area. *Collection Peter Boyd-Smith at Cobwebs*

Below A late view of the Quarter Deck pool showing the Magrodome in the closed position - it was usually in this position, except for Caribbean cruises and warm weather sectors of the World Cruise. The large white-backed chairs with plum upholstery replaced the sea-green, terry-towelling-covered, lightweight chairs in the 1992 Hamburg refit. This pool, 31 ft 6 in long by 22 feet wide was 6 feet at the deep end and 3 ft 6 in at the shallow end. It contained 17,000 gallons of water. *Terry Yarwood*

Right An early view of the One Deck pool area. Note the unrestricted aft end of the deck. Here passengers could look down and see the wake of the ship - an impressive sight, especially when crossing the Atlantic at up to 31 knots. No other form of transport can convey the vast distance involved in crossing from Southampton to New York - 116 hours of non-stop power, propelling QE2 relentlessly to her destination. Today, life rafts are in the aftmost position and are railed off, obstructing passengers from looking directly down to the sea below. *Cunard Archives, New York*

Below The Quarter Deck and One Deck pools, as well as the open expanse of deck space on the Sports Deck, are well illustrated in this view of QE2 during trials in the English Channel in 1969. Note the aft-facing windows of the Double Down Aft Bar on Upper Deck. The original funnel was painted white until 1982, when it appeared in traditional Cunard red with two black bands following the major changes as a result of QE2's sterling service in the Falklands Campaign in the South Atlantic. The funnel was replaced with a slightly fatter one, although of similar design, during the major re-engining in 1987. The new profile emphasised the characteristic Cunard markings, much to the joy of maritime purists. *Cunard Archives, New York*

Left The Magrodome viewed from Boat Deck. This structure added considerable weight to the aft section of QE2 and required regular cleaning, especially after transatlantic crossings. When not opened it created a greenhouse effect in the Club Lido below, so its removal has not been lamented. The golf-driving range in the foreground has been relocated following the 1994 changes. *Gary Buchanan*

Below left The expansive open decks were restored during the 1994 refit. In addition to the Magrodome, the support structures for the motorised tenders *Alpha* and *Beta* were removed. The unobstructed deck space, as seen here at Upper Deck aft - which forms the roof of the new Lido Cafe - gives much-needed room for sun-worshippers during warm weather cruising. The open decks aft are very popular at sail-away parties and deck stewards serve passengers from several temporary bars which are erected at strategic locations. *Gary Buchanan*

Above One Deck pool and Lido today. Jacuzzis were added in the 1987 refit and the whole pool and surrounds were re-tiled and covered in teak in 1994. This pool - one of only two left out of four passenger pools originally incorporated in 1969 - measures 29 feet long by 20 feet wide, and is 8 feet at the deep end and 3 ft 6 in at the shallow end. It contains 15,600 gallons of sea water, filtered through continually running sand filters. *Alan Chandler*

Above The Six Deck pool in 1969. Designed by Jon Bannenberg, he gave this area Glamrock walls and cantilevered seats, creating a feeling of warm stone, rather than creating a Roman Bath type of pool, full of white tiles and marble. Onlookers could see bathers through a tan-simulating screen of sepia glass. Circular red fibreglass changing booths were lined with Indian printed cotton, laminated into fibre-glass. Their curved backs protruded into the area occupied by the pool itself to give an even greater effect of warmth with glowing colour. The Turkish Baths were adjacent to the pool and there were masseurs in attendance during the day. The pool was 30 feet long and 18 feet wide, 6 feet at the deep end and 4 feet at the shallow end; it contained 17,500 gallons. *Cunard Archives, New York*

Above right The Six Deck pool was removed in the 1992 refit and Steiners of London created a magnificent state-of-the-art spa. In addition to the main thalassotherapy pool, there are French hydrotherapy baths, saunas, inhalation and steam rooms as well as seawater, Swedish and Shiatsu massage. Access is via the F stairway. *Niall Clutton/MET Studio Ltd, London*

Right The Seven Deck pool, by C stairway, was designed by Dennis Lennon. He achieved a sunny atmosphere using yellow Formica panelling and yellow and white floor tiles. There were saunas and a gymnasium on either side of the pool. The swimming pool remains today - a large pool, about the size of that on One Deck - but little else would remind today's visitors of the facilities that were offered in 1969 - state-of-the-art in their day, but basic by today's fitness-conscious standards. Steiners have created an all-encompassing, ultra-modern, hi-tech Cybex and Life-Cycle gymnasium, and a dedicated fitness team are on hand to instruct in personal fitness programmes, in addition to regular elementary and advanced aerobics classes. *Alan Chandler*

Above When commissioned, QE2 had a colour-coding to its stairways. One staircase had a light-blue balustrade with white walls (A stairway), originally designed for use by Tourist Class passengers - the lifts still don't stop at Quarter Deck or One Deck. Another had royal blue with dark blue leather walls and a white handrail (D stairway); this was designed to be the main First Class access point, and even today the lifts don't descend lower than Three Deck. A third had a brown motif with an orange handrail (E stairway), and this serves the entire ship from Five Deck to Boat Deck with four lifts, which are emergency powered. Another was in red russet brown with bright red handrails (G stairway), which serves as an access point aft with lifts operating from Five Deck to Upper Deck - in the 1994 refit the stairs were extended up to Boat Deck and allow inside access to the shopping level. During 1994 refit many of the colour schemes were painted to reflect a more pleasing aesthetic. Some fibre-glass balustrades were replaced with wooden handrails, and the wall coverings and royal maroon carpets hark back to a more gracious era, rekindling memories of the great 'Queens'.

Here D stairway looks magnificent as it sweeps down from Upper Deck to Quarter Deck at the entrance to the new Mauretania Restaurant. At Boat Deck level, D stairway is the imposing new location for two massive portraits. One is of Her Majesty Queen Elizabeth the Queen Mother, which was originally exhibited on the Cunarder *Queen Elizabeth*. The other is of Her Royal Highness Princess Elizabeth with Prince Philip, which was originally hung on board *Caronia*. *Alan Chandler*

Above right This magnificent model of the first *Mauretania* of 1907 dominated the D stairway on Quarter Deck. Arguably the most famous ship ever built, at 31,938 tons she was far and away the largest in the world in her day. She measured 790 feet and clipped almost a whole day off the Atlantic speed record. Her best passage before the First World War was 4 days, 10 hours, 51 minutes, at an average speed of 26.06 knots. QE2 made her fastest-ever eastbound transatlantic crossing between 17 and 22 July 1990. Under the command of Captain Robin Woodall, this greyhound of the Atlantic completed the crossing in 4 days, 6 hours, 57 minutes at an average speed of 30.16 knots. The *Mauretania* held the world record - or Blue Riband - for the fastest crossing for 22 years, dominating the North Atlantic passenger trade until she was scrapped in 1935. Now part of the Heritage Trail on board QE2, this splendid model is illuminated at night. *Niall Clutton/MET Studio Ltd, London*

Right Prior to the 1994 refit, the focal hub of D stairway lobby on Quarter Deck was graced by three tapestries by Helen Banynina Hernmarck. Created in a variety of wools, these impressive images, collectively 7 feet high by 21 feet long, depict the launching ceremony of QE2. Today these tapestries hang at the top of E stairway on Boat Deck. The regal carpet specially commissioned for QE2 was introduced in 1992. This stylish design was short-lived, as was a similar concept in the Midships Lobby. They were replaced during the 1994 refit and auctioned at the 1995 World Cruise Charity Country Fayre. Michael M. Rosenberg CBE is now the proud owner of these unique mementos of his many cruises, while Cunard improved its donation to the charity children's orphanage considerably. *Gary Buchanan*

The Midships Lobby was created by Dan Wallace and was so completely different from the traditional Cunard, or indeed any ship-board lobby, that it was considered possibly too dramatic. Dennis Lennon designed bright emerald green banquettes to be placed around the lower well. This was traditionally the First Class embarkation point to QE2, with the forward lobby at A stairway or the aft lobby at G stairway serving the Tourist Class passengers. Today all passengers embark QE2 - assuming there is a raised telescopic gantry as there is in New York and Southampton - at the Midships Lobby. *William H. Miller*

Dramatic is a description that could certainly be applied to the Midships Lobby today. The black leather wall coverings and surrounds were replaced during the 1994 transformation by bird's-eye maple panelling. Surrounding the circular entranceway are four large montage panels, commissioned in 1994 from the British artist Peter Sutton. These illustrate key developments of the history of the Cunard Line from the first crossing by a Cunard ship - the *Britannia* - in 1840, to the construction of QE2 on Clydebank in the late 1960s. A series of high-definition Linn Hi Fi speakers now allow recorded classical music to be played to dramatic effect throughout the day. *Alan Chandler*

Above left The Computer Learning Centre, forward on Two Deck, is now a very popular venue indeed. In the design stages this area was to be the Third Class Lobby and Purser's Office, but when launched this area was devoted to the Forward Lobby, containing the Bank and Purser's Office for Tourist Class passengers. Later these functions were amalgamated into the Purser's Office and Bank at Two Deck by the F stairway and the space became the Duty Free Liquor Shop. In the 1983 post-Falklands refit, a Computer Learning Centre was introduced. At this time it was located on Boat Deck, port side by the D stairway in what is now the Boardroom. Created in the 1987 refit, the enlarged Computer Learning Centre is busy by day and by night. *Gary Buchanan*

Left The Boardroom began as the London Gallery. Designed in 1969 by Stefan Buzas and operated by the Marlborough Fine Art Gallery of London, it showcased works by Graham Sutherland and Ben Nicholson. This venture did not last long, and by 1972 the London Gallery became the Reading Room with pale green lounge chairs and occasional tables. This tranquil retreat remained a popular venue with many passengers until 1983. Reflecting modern technology, this long room, with superb sea views, then became the Computer Learning and Video Centre. This in turn was moved to Two Deck by A stairway in the 1987 refit, and the Boat Deck room became the Boardroom and Business Centre. Today, during the World Cruise, it is devoted to members of the Samuel Cunard Key Club. *Collection R. W. Warwick*

Above The Upper Deck Library, on the port side between the D and E stairways, was designed by Dennis Lennon. A wonderful room, it enjoyed cathedral-like calm and was insulated from any noise emanating from the Theatre Bar. This large library, twice the size of today's library on Quarter Deck, boasted deep leather sofas with slatted blinds to counter a tropical sun. The bookshelves were lined with blue leather and a paler blue tweed was used in some of the chairs. No footsteps were heard on the thick-ribbed beige carpet, and there were bright, striped Conran fabrics at the windows. During the 1972 refit this most comfortable room was removed and the Players Club Casino and Lounge installed. *William H. Miller*

Above The Quarter Deck Library, again designed by Michael Inchbald, used a clever combination of brass and leather to create a nautical effect. Writing chairs were in brass and black leather while brass-bound ship's chests served as side tables with deep Chesterfields that evoked the smoking room atmosphere of the ships of yesteryear. This room remained relatively unchanged until the major rebuilding of Quarter Deck amidships during the 1994 refit. *Cunard Archives, New York*

Above right The Library and Bookshop today. The former now contains over 6,000 books in addition to over 700 videos for in-cabin use. There are also contemporary magazines and daily newspapers when available. The oil painting of *Cuba* by Samuel Walters is one of the finest maritime paintings owned by Cunard. In the bookshop nautical publications are on sale, as are the titles written by the many authors and celebrities who regularly lecture on board as part of the enrichment series presented on crossings and cruises. There are also lively book-signings when passengers meet with many famous writers, actors and adventurers. There is a separate room containing four CD-ROM computers and a multi-media library. In a central, glass-fronted cabinet is a selection of maritime memorabilia for sale. This is supplied from the treasure-trove of artefacts and collectors items to be found at Cobwebs in Northam Road, Southampton. To this day QE 2 is the only ship afloat with not just one, but two professional librarians, offering friendly and helpful advice to passengers. *Alan Chandler*

Right The original Card Room, designed by Jon Bannenberg, had wall panels and chairs in green suede to complement the green baize tops of the rosewood tables, while a deep green and beige speckled carpet completed this popular room on Quarter Deck, just forward of the Library on the port side. It underwent a few cosmetic changes over the many refits, but the most drastic change came in 1994 when the space was devoted to the new Bookshop. *Terry Yarwood*

The Players Club Casino and Hideaway Lounge on Upper Deck, forward on the port side, installed in the 1972 refit, were greatly enlarged and remodelled during the 1990 Hamburg refit. Designed by Graham Fayhe, this room has a most dignified ambience - especially around the four Black Jack tables and Baccarat table, recessed in an alcove with Art Deco etched glass and impressionist murals of life on board the *Queen Mary*. The slot machines and poker machines are in use day and night on many cruises, with play only usually interrupted for the regular Bingo sessions held most afternoons in the Grand Lounge - conveniently located just aft of the Casino. *Cunard, New York*

The Theatre, or multi-purpose auditorium as it was called in 1969, was designed by Gaby Schreiber & Associates for use as a church, conference hall, theatre and cinema. The main auditorium was constructed of pre-formed fibre-glass panelling, which also covered the projection room. The stage area was left open, but panels flanking the stage were pivoted to form wings from adjacent dressing-room areas. Seating 500, each armchair seat had a fold-down table for conference use and a pocket containing a short-wave receiver for use when simultaneous translations were in operation.

The seating has been changed on two occasions but little else. The Captain holds an interdenominational church service every Sunday at sea, as does the on-board Priest who celebrates Mass. Latest-release movies are shown at fixed times throughout the day and night. Passengers can either sit in the lower, main section on Upper Deck or in the balcony, which is accessed from the D stairway on Boat Deck. *Collection R. W. Warwick*

Professor Mischa Black, from the Royal College of Art, designed the Synagogue. Located on Three Deck at the A stairway, this place of worship for passengers of the Jewish faith is peacefully decorated in blue with ash panels. Originally the main (Columbia) galley had a separate kosher kitchen, which conformed to the highest standards of Kashruth, but this was removed in the 1987 refit. Today the Synagogue remains completely unchanged; it is the sole public space on board QE2 that is in its original design. *Gary Buchanan*

Wednesday, January 1, 1969

R.M.S. "QUEEN ELIZABETH 2"

Captain W.E. Warwick, Officers and Ship's Company, wish you all A Very Happy New Year

The Guinea Pig Exercise is now completed. We should like to thank all passengers for their co-operation in helping us to try out the various public rooms, their constructive suggestions and for completing the various feedback forms. Despite the difficult circumstances a vast amount of information has been obtained from these exercises which will prove of the greatest value to the ship on her commercial voyages.

For your guidance, the following areas are available for use today:

All Open Decks
Sports Deck: Children's Playroom
Boat Deck: 736 Club, Theatre Balcony, Juke Box
Upper Deck: Theatre Stalls, Library and Theatre Bar
Quarter Deck: Card Room, Queens Room, Q4 Room
Midships Bar

Your Six-Channel receiver will be programmed today as follows:
Channel 1 — Continuous background music
Channel 2 — 10.00 a.m. to Noon and 4.00 p.m. to 6.00 p.m. Light Classical Music
Channel 3 — News Broadcast — each hour on the hour
Channel 4 — B.B.C. Radio Four
Channel 5 — B.B.C. Radio One
Channel 6 — Recorded classical concerts as programmed below

Visits to the Bridge have been arranged as follows:
2.30 p.m. 376-450 / 3.00 p.m. 451-525 / 3.30 p.m. 526-600
Please meet outside the 736 Club at 'A' Staircase on the Boat Deck

From 7.00 a.m.— Swimming Pool available — Six Deck (Use F staircase elevator, parents MUST accompany children)

8.00 a.m. Holy Communion will be celebrated in the Upper Deck Library (Communicant members of the Free Churches are welcome)

8.00 a.m. Breakfast served:
Britannia Restaurant: 1-300 and 701-870
Columbia Restaurant: 301-600 and 901-970

9.00 a.m. to 6.30 p.m.— Children's Playroom available on Sports Deck

10.00 a.m. Theatre reserved for Press Conference (901-970)

10.00 a.m. Attention Children! A morning with Uncle Reg Deck Hike, followed by lots of Fun and Games

10.15 a.m. Look Lively! (Meet Bryan Vickers in the Theatre Bar for a brisk walk on deck followed by some simple exercises)

10.30 a.m. Coffee served (voluntary) Queens Room

10.30 p.m. Q4 Room is reserved for the Press

10.30 a.m. Recorded Concert — Channel 6 "Il Tabarro" Opera in one Act (Sung in Italian) (Libretto by Guiseppe Adami) Orchestra of the Opera House Rome. Section of the Chorus of the Opera House, Rome. (Chorus Master: Guiseppe Conca). Conducted by Vincenzo Bellezza. Recorded in the Opera House, Rome (Puccini)

11.00 a.m. Miss Maureen Ryan continues her talk on places of interest in London — Theatre

11.15 a.m. Come along and join the Westleys for the Final Dance Class in the Theatre Bar

Noon Cocktail Time — Your choice of rendezvous: 736 Club, Theatre Bar (Nina Midgley entertains on the Piano) Midships Bar and Q4 Room

1.00 p.m. Luncheon served:
Britannia Restaurant: 183-450 and 701-870
Columbia Restaurant: 1-100; 451-600 and 901-970
Grill: 101-182

2.15 p.m. Children's Film Show — Playroom

2.30 p.m. Whist Drive (Prizes) — Q4 Room

4.15 p.m. Todays Movie in the Theatre "Nobody Runs Forever" featuring Rod Taylor Christopher Plummer and Camilla Sparv Running Time: 1 hour, 41 minutes; Cert. 'A'

4.30 p.m. Roman Catholic Holy Mass will be said in the Upper Deck Library

5.00 p.m. Attention Children! Rhythm Band — Queens Room (Instrument and Tuition provided)

5.00 p.m. Recorded Concert — Channel 6 Symphony No.4 in D Minor Op.120. The Philharmonia Orchestra conducted by Guido Cantelli (Schumann)

5.00 p.m. Look-Out Reserved for Press (901-970)

6.00 p.m. Cocktail Time — Your choice of rendezvous Q4 Room; Theatre Bar (Nina Midgley entertains on the Piano)

6.00 p.m. Midships Bar reserved for the Press

6.30 p.m. Children's High Tea — Britannia Restaurant (Compulsory 1 to 10 years inclusive)

7.15 p.m. Attention Children! A programme of short films will be shown in the Playroom

7.30 p.m. Dinner served (INFORMAL)
Britannia Restaurant: 165-400 and 701-870
Columbia Restaurant: 1-164 and 401-600
Grill: 901-970

Movie Time in the Theatre:

9.30 p.m. "Becket" featuring Richard Burton and Peter O'Toole Running Time: 2 hours, 29 minutes; Cert. 'A'

In the Queens Room from 9.15 p.m. to 1.00 a.m.
FINAL BINGO SESSION (Phillips presentation gift tonight is a Cassette Tape Player)
followed by
Farewell Dance and Revue
Revue at 10.30 p.m. features
Ann Emery; The Westleys:
Lori and the Wells Brothers:
Russ Clevedon and the New Sound
El Payo and the Spanish Dancers
Edmund Hockridge
(Dancing to the Music of Basil Stutely and his Orchestra featuring Annette Roberts)

In the Theatre Bar tonight:
From 10.00 p.m. to 1.00 a.m.— Nina Midgley entertains on the Piano

In the Q4 Room tonight:
From 10.00 p.m. to 3.00 a.m.— Dancing to the Swining Rhythm of the Dougie Ward Trio
Cabaret at 12.30 a.m. featuring Russ Clevedon and the New Sound

In the 736 Club tonight:
From 10.00 p.m. to 2.00 a.m.— Disco Time with Diane, Ming and Vanessa

NOTICES

Expense Claims
All Guinea Pig passengers (1-600 701-870) are requested to bring their Special Expenses Claim Form to the Tour Office for settlement today, as follows:
2.00 p.m. to 3.00 p.m. — Nos. 1-200
3.00 p.m. to 4.00 p.m. — Nos. 201-400
4.00 p.m. to 5.00 p.m. — Nos. 401-600
5.00 p.m. to 6.00 p.m. — Nos. 701-870
The Press (901-970) are requested to visit the Tour Office at 10.00 a.m. on Thursday

Baggage should be packed and ready for removal from Staterooms by 8.30 a.m.
Luncheon will be served at 12.30 p.m.
QE2 is expected to arrive alongside the Ocean Terminal, Southampton at 1 p.m. Thursday, 2nd January and disembarkation will commence from the Rotunda "2" Deck shortly afterwards
H.M. Immigration inspection for passengers who embarked at Las Palmas will be held in the Card Room, Quarter Deck, at 1.15 p.m.

Cabaret presented by arrangement with Bernard Delfont Ltd.
Orchestras by Geraldo of London

Above QE2's daily programme from 1 January 1969, the last day at sea for QE2's first 'cruise' to the Canary Islands before returning to Southampton. On arrival there were no welcoming bands and no civic reception. This 'Guinea Pig Cruise' was a great disappointment to Cunard. It would be five months before QE2 sailed on her inaugural transatlantic crossing from Southampton. Problems with the turbines delayed delivery, with Cunard refusing to accept the ship from Upper Clyde Shipbuilders (by that time John Brown's parent company). QE2 entered commercial service on 22 April 1969 with a short shakedown cruise to the Canary Islands. One thousand voyages later the daily programme is a wealth of information.

Right The daily programme from the 1,000th voyage of QE2 from New York to Southampton on 14 June 1995. Every day this comprehensive guide to what's on is delivered to each cabin. It is the responsibility of the Cruise Director and his staff to ensure that the plethora of activities available each day, as well as restaurant information and bar hours, are highlighted in this most useful ship-board agenda.

Wednesday, 14th June, 1995
In Port of: NEW YORK
Sunrise: 5.22am Sunset: 8.22pm

Dress Code This Evening:
INFORMAL—JACKET & TIE REQUIRED

CUNARD

Queen Elizabeth 2

DAILY PROGRAMME

CAPTAIN JOHN BURTON-HALL,
the OFFICERS and CREW
welcome you aboard
for the historical 1000th VOYAGE of
Queen Elizabeth 2

We hope that this will be a relaxing holiday and an exciting experience for you as Queen Elizabeth 2 crosses the Atlantic to Southampton arriving on Monday, 19th June.

FESTIVE SAILAWAY
At 2.45pm,
Upper Deck Aft,
CELEBRATE!
with a glass of Champagne, compliments of Cunard Line.
Music by
THE QE2 ORCHESTRA
under the direction of
Ray Price-Evans.

Artwork By: Simon Davey, Crew Supervisor
Printed Onboard By: The QE2 Print Shop

Cruise Director: BRIAN PRICE
Social Director: ANDREW GRAHAM

Captain: JOHN BURTON-HALL

Deputy Cruise Director: ANGELA BEHRENS
Social Directress: MAUREEN RYAN

Above Before the installation of the penthouses, the cabins on One and Two Decks were the highest-grade accommodations available on QE 2. Forty-six of the cabins amidships had intercommunicating doors to adjoining cabins to form suites. The port-side suite - known originally as the Schreiber Suite - contained two twin and one single cabins. There were originally four different colour schemes in the First Class cabins: red, orange, pale blue, and white and yellow ochre. Timber veneers in rosewood, ash and cedar were extensively employed on the walls. Each cabin was air-conditioned (unlike those of the earlier 'Queens'), had a telephone (there were two telephone operators manning the switchboard in 1969), toilet and bath and/or shower, with a console controlling six channels of radio programmes and the cabin lights. Suite rooms were created by a number of designers and some incorporated beds that could be converted into a settee by day. There were originally no double beds on QE 2 - two single beds would be pushed together. Some of these deluxe accommodations boasted ceilings in timber panelling in Swiss Pear with velvet wall panelling and silk curtains. *Cunard Archives, New York*

Above right Today the One and Two Deck ultra-deluxe, Queen's Grill grade cabins are extremely spacious and reflect an understated elegance in their interior decorations and fabrics. *Alan Chandler*

Right During the 1994 refit nearly all the bathrooms on board QE 2 were modernised, and the marble opulence found in many of the One and Two Deck bathrooms offers, in addition to copious closets, great space - a commodity noticeable by its absence on modern cruise ships. *Niall Clutton/MET Studio Ltd, London*

Left When the first 20 penthouses were added at the Vosper Thorneycroft refit in Southampton in 1972, a new dimension in luxurious accommodations was added to QE2. This Sports Deck suite, with its own private veranda, reflects the Seventies design, so much in vogue in that era. *Cunard Archives, New York*

Above An identical penthouse suite, 23 years on. The appointments and finish have been considerably improved to provide incomparable luxury on the high seas. *Alan Chandler*

Left Styled with ingenuity and flair by top designers from Britain and America, the two duplex suites - the Trafalgar Suite and the Queen Anne suite - were innovative in their lavish appointments. The Trafalgar Suite sitting room shown here boasted dressing rooms, a private cocktail bar with refrigerator, and two bathrooms - it was designed to resemble Lord Nelson's quarter's on HMS *Victory*. A stairway leads up to the bedroom on Signal Deck, port side. *Cunard Archives, New York*

Below left Several of the original penthouses were equipped with Murphy beds, which could fold away by day - as seen on the left of this view - giving a very large lounge area for entertaining or simply to luxuriate in. *Cunard Archives, New York*

Above The Queen Anne Suite - the starboard duplex suite - was originally furnished in the style and period of the name it bears, but the decor was changed to more soothing pastel shades during the 1987 refit. *Cunard Archives, London*

Even the penthouse corridor exudes an opulent air. Reached by a series of stairs or lift from the Queen's Grill Lounge, QE2 now boasts no fewer than 34 penthouse suites. This corridor leads forward to the ultimate in opulence - the split-level Queen Elizabeth and Queen Mary suites, complete with private conservatories and forward-facing verandas. *Alan Chandler*

Passengers in penthouse accommodation are pampered by day and by night. Butler service is all part of the service, and Geoffrey Coughtrey is one of the last British stewards in the old tradition - a veteran of the second *Mauretania*, the *Caronia*, the *Queen Mary* and the *Franconia*. From the maiden voyage of QE2, Geoffrey has smoothed the passage of the rich and famous, from Eleanor Roosevelt and Cary Grant to the Duke and Duchess of Windsor. He has washed a contessa's diamonds in gin every night - at her behest - and made a miniature life jacket for one lady passenger's pet pigeon - all part of life's rich tapestry in the rarefied atmosphere of the most prestigious penthouses on the high seas. *Alan Chandler*

Above In 1972 the shops on Boat Deck, between D and E stairways, were relocated aft to the balcony of the Double Up Room. This made space for ten more ultra-deluxe cabins to be built. They offer superb views on to the promenade Boat Deck and are very popular with repeat passengers. *Cunard Archives, London*

Above right In addition to the 46 luxury suite rooms, QE2 also had 245 deluxe rooms when commissioned in 1969. The number of deluxe rooms has since been increased through continual upgrading following the introduction of the Queen's Grill in 1972 and the Princess Grill Starboard (now the Britannia Grill) in 1990. *Cunard Archives, New York*

Right As this view shows, little has changed in layout between the original design and the interiors enjoyed by today's passengers. In this Princess Grill-grade cabin furnishings have become more subtle, with matching, restful fabrics, new televisions and video recorders, as well as personal amenities such as hair dryers and in-cabin safes. *Niall Clutton/McNeece Ltd, London*

This view shows a refurbished bathroom for a Caronia Restaurant C3-grade cabin following the 1994 refit. The marble surrounds give the vanity units a luxurious feel rarely found on cruise ships today. *Niall Clutton/MET Studio Ltd, London*

Right Tourist Class cabins were again designed in red, orange, pale blue, and white and yellow ochre, and, like the First Class cabins, had four different colour schemes for cushions and bed spreads with curtains in a wool-tweed material. There were combinations of yellow-gold, blue and green, brown and yellow, pink and orange or red, and white and black. This two-bed cabin on Four Deck is a good example of the many popular options available in 1969. *Cunard Archives, New York*

Below A similar cabin today. The fabrics might be less gaudy, but there is still a good deal of space. This C4-grade cabin is assigned to passengers dining in the Caronia Restaurant. *Cunard Archives, New York*

The standard Four and Five Deck cabins when QE2 sailed on her maiden voyage provided all creature comforts - wall-to-wall carpeting, adjustable heat controls, multi-channel radio as well as enough drawer and closet space to satisfy any traveller in this Britannia Restaurant (now Mauretania Restaurant) grade inside cabin. The plaid fabrics were replaced during the late 1970s and a lighter interior decor introduced. *Cunard Archives, New York*

Right An outside, Mauretania minimum-grade cabin today. Note the upper bed neatly tucked away. Even this economy cabin has television and enjoys twice-daily steward/stewardess service in addition to 24-hour room service. *Niall Clutton/McNeece Ltd, London*

Left These M3 grade cabins have a shower rather than a bath, but, as seen here, the new appointments, added during the 1994 refit, make an economical and efficient use of the space. Note the marble on the vanity unit - just the same as in the deluxe-grade cabins. *Niall Clutton/MET Studio Ltd, London*

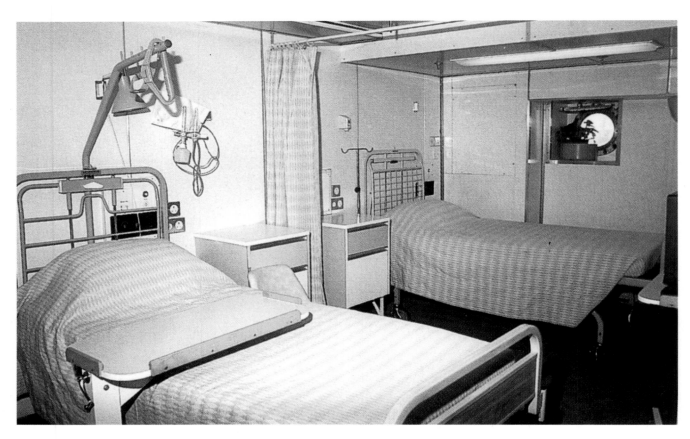

One bed few passengers wish to sleep in! Consisting of four multi-bed wards and one single-bed ward, QE2's hospital contains a total of 13 beds. Situated on Six Deck by the C stairway (or C-Six for short), medical care of the highest standard is provided by two fully qualified doctors and three nurses. There is also an operating theatre, laboratory, lead-lined X-ray room, fully equipped dental-care unit (for use on the World Cruise) and a physiotherapy ward. *Collection R. W. Warwick*

QE2 is a transatlantic car ferry capable of carrying 12 cars. It is for this reason that the RAC was able to award QE2 Five Stars - the only ship that could ever have such a prestigious accolade bestowed upon it, since a criterion for this highest echelon is a requirement for covered parking for at least ten vehicles. The drive on-drive off facilities fore and aft can be used depending on the state of the tide. Special lifts, capable of carrying 5-ton loads, were installed in QE2 back in 1969 - one is located by A stairway, the other by H stairway, descending to the holds on Seven and Eight Decks. There is a turntable to facilitate the stowage and removal of vehicles via the ramps, which can be used at New York, Southampton and Cherbourg. *Collection R. W. Warwick*

Above The massive bow of QE2 dwarfs dockside victualling equipment. The forward ramp that can be seen is used for taking supplies on board, and the car ramp is slightly aft of this. Turnaround time for QE2 at Southampton can be as short as 6 hours - no mean feat to land up to 1,854 passengers and their baggage and embark the same number with many pieces of luggage, not to mention the myriad of supplies required by the Hotel Department. *Niall Clutton/MET Studio Ltd, London*

Top Captain John Burton-Hall RD, Cdr RNR was appointed Master of QE2 in October 1994, following the retirement of Captain Robin A. Woodall RD, RNR. He was first appointed Captain of QE2 on 7 March 1990. *Alan Chandler*

Middle The Relief Captain of QE2 is Ronald W. Warwick Lt Cdr RNR, FNI - his first appointment as Captain was on 26 July 1990. His father, Commodore William E. Warwick CBE, RD, RNR was the first Master of QE2; officially appointed on 23 December 1968, he retired in 1972. *Collection R. W. Warwick*

Bottom The author standing at the new controls on the starboard wing of the Bridge. This book is Gary Buchanan's second about this great ship, *Dream Voyages* having been published in 1989. He is a very regular passenger on board and lectures about the history of QE2 as part of the on-board enrichment programme. *Gary Buchanan*

Index

Brooks
Hutchi
(Sou
Lloyd
Con
Maxto
Year
Miller,
(Lor
Moxo
- Cu

d, Frost, Jack, *The Queen Elizabeth 2*
)69)
id St John, *The Cunard Book of*
evon, 1990)
nald W., *QE2 - The Cunard Line*
merset 1993)
iam M., *QE2 - The Official Pictorial*
lifornia, 1988)

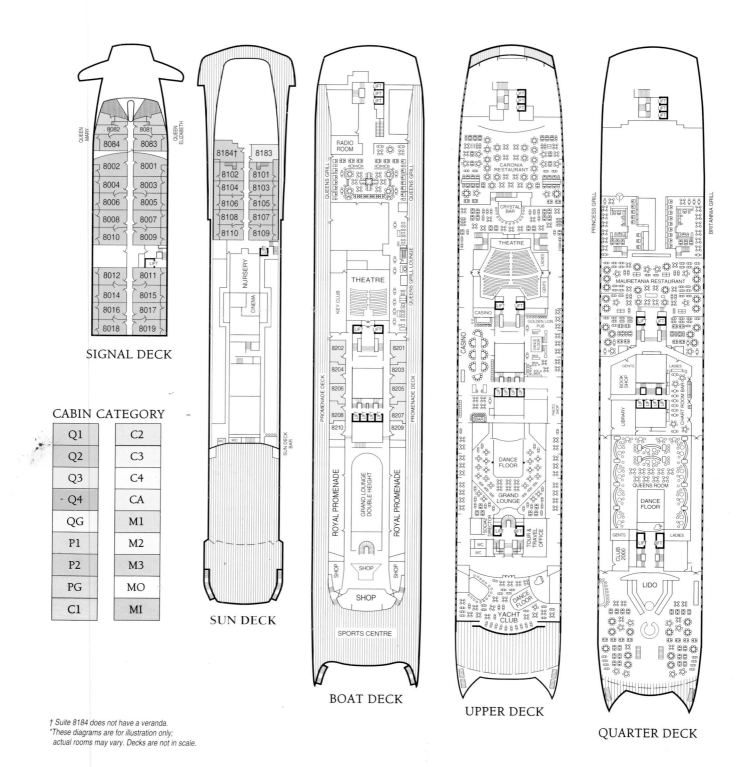

SIGNAL DECK

8082 | 8081
8084 | 8083
8002 | 8001
8004 | 8003
8006 | 8005
8008 | 8007
8010 | 8009
8012 | 8011
8014 | 8015
8016 | 8017
8018 | 8019

QUEEN MARY   QUEEN ELIZABETH

LIFT

SUN DECK

8184† | 8183
8102 | 8101
8104 | 8103
8106 | 8105
8108 | 8107
8110 | 8109

NURSERY

CINEMA

WC | WC

SUN DECK BAR

CABIN CATEGORY

Q1	C2
Q2	C3
Q3	C4
Q4	CA
QG	M1
P1	M2
P2	M3
PG	MO
C1	MI

BOAT DECK

RADIO ROOM

QUEENS GRILL | QUEENS GRILL

QUEENS GRILL LOUNGE

THEATRE

KEY CLUB

8202 | 8201
8204 | 8203
8206 | 8205
8208 | 8207
8210 | 8209

LIFT | LIFT

PROMENADE DECK | PROMENADE DECK

ROYAL PROMENADE | ROYAL PROMENADE

GRAND LOUNGE DOUBLE HEIGHT

SHOP | SHOP

SHOP

SHOP

SPORTS CENTRE

WC | WC

UPPER DECK

LIFT

CARONIA RESTAURANT

CRYSTAL BAR

THEATRE

CASINO

LIFT | LIFT

GOLDEN LION PUB

LADIES

GENTS

DANCE FLOOR

CASINO

BAR

PHOTO SHOP

DANCE FLOOR

GRAND LOUNGE

SOCIAL DIRECTOR

TOUR & TRAVEL OFFICE

WC | WC

YACHT CLUB

DANCE FLOOR

QUARTER DECK

LIFT | LIFT

PRINCESS GRILL | BRITANNIA GRILL

MAURETANIA RESTAURANT

LIFT | LIFT

GENTS | LADIES

BOOK SHOP

LIBRARY

CHART ROOM BAR

QUEENS ROOM

DANCE FLOOR

GENTS | LADIES

LIFT | LIFT

CLUB 2000

LIDO

† Suite 8184 does not have a veranda.
*These diagrams are for illustration only; actual rooms may vary. Decks are not in scale.

BOAT DECK
QUARTER DECK
TWO DECK
FOUR DECK
SIX DECK

SIGNAL DECK
SUN DECK
UPPER DECK
ONE DECK
THREE DECK
FIVE DECK
SEVEN DECK